A
Little
Resurrection

Also by Selina Nwulu

Keep the Bodies Buried
The Secrets I Let Slip

A
Little
Resurrection

SELINA
NWULU

BLOOMSBURY POETRY

LONDON · OXFORD · NEW YORK · NEW DELHI · SYDNEY

BLOOMSBURY POETRY
Bloomsbury Publishing Plc
50 Bedford Square, London, WC1B 3DP, UK
29 Earlsfort Terrace, Dublin 2, Ireland

BLOOMSBURY, BLOOMSBURY POETRY and the Diana logo
are trademarks of Bloomsbury Publishing Plc

First published in Great Britain 2022

A catalogue record for this book is available from the British Library

ISBN: PB: 978-1-5266-4998-0; eBook: 978-1-5266-4997-3;
ePDF: 978-1-5266-4996-6

2 4 6 8 10 9 7 5 3 1

Typeset by Laura Jones
Printed and bound in Great Britain by
CPI Group (UK) Ltd, Croydon CR0 4YY

To find out more about our authors and books
visit www.bloomsbury.com and sign up for our newsletters

CONVERSATIONS AT THE BUS STOP: ANGEL

I've been an angel before. No big deal, but it's true. I've held a man as he lay dying. You never know, do you? How you'll feel when you know it's the end. That day, the rest of us had nothing left to do but turn celestial. Morph ourselves into a choir of angels, singing Amazing Grace, and in that moment, I suppose it was an amazing passage, awful too. Have you ever thought about it like that? Anastasia, an older woman I once danced with, said when a parent dies the best you can do is to ensure things are as comfortable for them as possible, her eyes dulled from knowing. There may be no room for the words that have been pickling in the roof of your mouth. To be an angel is a holy burden, means to soothe, give without taking. She twirled me around, spun me until I fell by his hospital bed, watching him fade like an Etch-A-Sketch, more pallid with his every shake. I sat there stunned, swallowing my feelings like pellets. An angel trying to make everything as easy as possible. Selfless, that's me – meaning a part of me became less that day. Now I leave all my doors open, waiting for my return.

At the funeral, mourners said she had her father's lips
as if she'd plucked them from the open coffin and stitched
them to her face. How the lips now puppet the words

it's what he would have wanted despite the storms
in her stomach. How taut to truth they've become.
They will not let her rage speak here. Sorrow knocks

and the lips do not answer. When no one is watching
she peels the lips off her face like skin from a hardened
orange, watching them shrivel and blacken in her palm.

KEEP THE BODIES BURIED

I

When you tell me of your travels in the US,

you paint scenes of delirious road trips with the soft-top down
                        hands skimming coastal winds

hair blown back in whimsy
                    and lovers beguiling and wild like the landscapes.

You think me paranoid
        for mentioning black and brown lives
                            the cheap ricochet of blue bullets

        seems you've only ever known law like swing jazz
                        offbeat, and subject to improvisation.

        You demand
                    proof, motive, a reasonable explanation.

Do you know we are standing at the crossroads of our first fight?
                    We can stay here a little longer

but I will not dig up the graves of the taken, plunge spade
    through the ground to drag out corpses,
and line them up in front of you. I will not make their horror
    your pantomime, resuscitate them back to agony
and press your ear into the splutter of their last words,

the drool of their shock. I will not play them over
and over and over so you believe them.

II

The police came quick, met my screams
with the wail of their sirens.
Didn't need to knock – the door
hung jilted, kicked off its hinges.
They asked what the men took,
who and what I saw.

I did not say:
a black man who seemed scared
a black man with eyes like mine

I kept the facts plain.
Enough it seemed for the quickness
of tongues uttering well-worn descriptors,
skimmed stones across radio waves.
Police directives to hound the local area
for every black man, the ceremony of hot grip
and pat down, palms yanked into backward
prayer and handcuffs.

Black men with eyes like mine
frisked and shoved and I wonder whether
they will resist, or make their limbs and minds
malleable as bodies coming to the end of breath,
like the dead waiting to be buried.

The police left me in the kitchen,
a lone silhouette, unsure
what to hope for.

REPATRIATION I

Jimmy Aldaoud

was deported to Iraq and, upon dying sixty-three days later,
is returned and buried in US soil. His name, trigger
to a removal order, keen and precise as a bullet to the jugular.
A pawn picked up and dropped, proving nothing but the game
we've become, and this war is continuing. A bitter homecoming,
citizen to the flag only in dying; Jimmy, finally an American,

great again.

SOFTBOI COLUMBUS

He's one of the good ones
because after the theft
he'll order you an Uber home.
Behold Softboi Columbus!
who even knows words like *intersectionality*
and how to woo you with a bell hooks quote.
You're just *so interesting*,
possibly the most interesting thing about him.
How should one solve racism? he muses.
And what of the black community
after the Tottenham riots –
or should that be 'uprisings'?
A little repartee over dinner,
though he barely listens to your replies,
he's just staring at your lips.
Could you teach him how to cook jollof?
Take him dancing sometime?
Watch him watch your hips, the lustre of sweat
beading his brow for every sway.
Last thing at night, with his hands
around your throat, he remembers his lineage
and you his dark continent all along,
waiting to be tamed. He calls you *brown sugar*,
wants you, his *Nubian queen*,
to pour yourself into him,
dissolve sweetly on his tongue.

GOOD GIRL

Tag that follows me around like a skittering dog, panting
at my heels. Reward, I realise, for when I am silent enough.

Today I almost forgot I was a woman until I saw a man,
his jaw unhinging like a snake's, a tongue dull and long

slithering towards my chest. I found myself more girl-like,
unsure of myself. A girl gone good, just like he wanted.

FISHERMEN AT
OUAKAM BEACH, DAKAR

You do not fight the sun at its fiercest
rather bow down to its gift and rest.
I discover this on the beach in Dakar surrounded
by newfound uncles, fishermen stopping for lunch
who have made me, a passerby, a plate
without asking. My strangeness is no threat,
but a novelty, and I am enjoying the company
of men I do not fear, but could even love.
They offer *attaya, carpe rouge*, instructions
for who I should marry, their advice loud
and frolicking like waves, at odds and in sync
with each other's rhythm. I do not resist but swim
in them, allow myself to be swept from one wisecrack
to another. I am in awe of how much the landscape
wants them, extends its hospitality through the sun,
its rays an opening blossom seeking only
to fortify their blackness, the two-tier blue
of sky and sea illuminating the contours
of their silhouettes. How their feet, beach-ashen
and shallow-buried, become roots as the sand
surrenders to the weight of them.

When conversation turns to where I live,
whether they should move or send a son,
I watch a question mark emerge from each face.
I want them to stay here, in this moment,
though I have no right to say it, perhaps
even think it. But I know uncles who live

under grey skies, their skin more ghostly
for every bitter month, the way the landscape
turns each uncle into a warning, a hard body
with hands considered too big. I imagine
how the timbre of their voices might sound
delayed, echoing through choppy telephone
signal as if passing through the oceans
themselves. How they might say *it is well,*
no right to complain, the third of the money
they would live on, sending the rest back home.
And I remember the first time I saw my father
back in Nigeria, how much lighter
he looked. I didn't recognise him.

MY DAD'S JACKET LIVES ON
IN A POP-UP BAR IN SHOREDITCH

His glasses too, floating on the bearded face of a hipster;
wide aviators with a double bridge. Fickle reincarnation
turns studious into fashionable in a span of mere decades.
The jacket that once held the man washing the car
after church, now swoons in a beer garden asking me for a light.
I say nothing, because I don't want the jacket to know
I'd ever smoked – ever. *Where would one even buy a light?*
I want to say loudly. Do the pockets grieve?
Wish they were still carrying foiled sheets of aspirin,
hardened gum wrapped in tissue paper,
a wayward toothpick? Does the lining still look for him?
The arm of the jacket moves to greet a friend.
Instinctively I duck for cover.

DANDELION

Grief is a metallic thug numbing your tongue,
so let the razor speak to your scalp. Remind yourself
you too are capable of shedding, of leaving yourself behind.

Let it all fall, mother, let your hair drift away
until you are the bald stalk of a dandelion,
your wishes like downy tufts, blown elsewhere.

SAFEKEEPING

My mother has passed on her war,
swallowed stories too dangerous
to leave on her tongue, birthed
them into my core for safekeeping,
the body, Biafra's hiding place.

No wonder I dream of slaughterhouses,
wake up choking, my teeth rimmed
metallic with gunpowder. Why the tips
of my fingers feel haunted.

My mother has passed on her war.
Her memories have run their nails
through my insides. That I might know
I come from a lineage of long prayer
and fears I have no weapons for.

THE BLOOD AND THE WATER

The day I couldn't pronounce
the name of the Igbo man calling on the phone,
guilt spread like a thickening bruise,
the Englishness of my voice judging him.
My father couldn't look me in the face.

How many parents discover the pain
of raising foreigners who do not belong to them?
Children returning to their parents with shame
written across their faces when they discover
what the country must think of their blood.

It is a hate they do not own, but still
they become carriers of this disdain. This foreign
land is their inheritance now and so must
come the ritual of denial, of spitting out
their parents' languages like bitter leaf.

Every night a parent cries a heavenly plea
that their children may know their blood better
than the water, which can deceive and drown.
Is there a trip *back home* long enough?
A prayer more powerful than the slurs
sneaking through the crack under the door?

A HISTORY OF BANNING
(after Executive Order 13769)

they banned us from our countries banned us from theirs till
the earth became too scorched with eviction they banned us
from our bodies left us dismembered until we were heads bob-
bing on trees lungs flowered by gas injections sliced ears flung
across a field they banned us from our labour wrung our sweat
into water fountains we could not drink from they banned us
from our classrooms splintered our minds spun gibberish out of
our wisdoms banned us from our tongues made our languages
a deadweight swinging in the back of our throats spiked our
voices heavy with grief they banned us from praise locked our
names in quarantine to wither under sun they banned us from
shops from our clothes our garments spoke a beaten birdsong
banned us from our lovers threw the light of our laughter into
fire they banned us from burial stripped us of ritual and quest
they banned us from wonder what haven't they banned us from?
what won't we take back?

YESTERDAY WAS A FULL MOON AND
I DID NOT THINK OF DYING

A plane flew above my head and I thought of each body
on board, blew them a wish of ease and safety.

A tourist caught me in her picture, my face
living in the fabric of her memory.

I revisited an old wound, washed it clean
of my shame and at long last forgave myself.

I was run-down sick and got better. I marvelled at how many
    times
my body comes back to me, more sincerely than any lover.

The mirror was not my enemy and I did not bare teeth
but held my own gaze, blessed every bump and curve.

I have made a home in the space between being loved and
    alone, have shaken off its contradictions;

*Today I am grateful to be alone and to be deeply loved,
the former does not cancel the latter.*

In the end, when I scatter wide the pieces of my life,
I will honour it, feast upon the bitter and the sweet, and give
    thanks.

PRAYER FOR THE DEPORTED

Protest didn't work for Jimmy Mubenga
on a flight just like this one,
his words, *you're killing me*, wrestling
through the aisle. No one responded
until the quiet shell of him lay
slumped. Your body is also caged
between security guards armed
with nothing to lose, so do not make a fuss;
virtue has never been given
to the banished. When a flight attendant
approaches, look for the smile in their eyes.
Drink the water, ruminate over the choice
of one ice cube or two. Chicken or fish.
Let the A/C wish you well, cool you
into the long hours of turbulence.
For this moment, pretend you are like
everyone else flying in this vessel, soaring
over terrain from this height, small
and insignificant, flitting through a harbour
of clouds, its own kingdom, and you,
part of a hopeful congregation, where,
at last, your flesh and bones are enough.

HALF-WRITTEN LOVE LETTER

My parents came here after hearing the seas
of the British Isles, as if they put their ears
to its shell and the waves threw themselves tipsy
against conch, willing them to come over.

Then there were the things
we understood without words;

how the sun in these parts is a slow swell,
the coastal walks of Dundee,
graffiti hieroglyphics, damp shoes
against Sheffield cobbles and
the tastebud clench of a tart apple.

We learnt this country fiercely,
my father felt its knuckles crush his jaw,
my mother delivered its children.
I have been kissed deeply by its tongue,
it has licked Yorkshire on my vowels,
I am a half-written love letter
I do not know where to send.

So when *go home* becomes
a neighbourhood war cry,
we understand we are not what you wanted,
have been written clean out of your folklores.
But we have built here, loved here, died here,
already carry the heartache of leaving.
When we go home, we go back reeking of you.

Windrush is a dirty word now; all burden,
hostile and foreign – so the deportations.

Guests spat out now the rebuilding is done,
and what welcome awaits a return so haggard?

Familiar buildings frail and replaced, old flames
that have learned to love without them, hurricanes vengeful,

more merciless than they used to be. How long does it take
to find their old tongues? To ask themselves, *was it worth*

what I gave? Was any of it ever really enough?
and not know what language to reply in.

HOW TO SPEAK TO GOD

There are certain things I cannot kneel down and pray for;
thoughts longing and unholy, that smell like three a.m.
and stale beer the morning after. If prayers could seek guidance
for anything, I might have said yes to a tall stranger's smile
on a crisp night no one else was watching.

But church life runs deep and prayers for protection
cannot be dirty, must not drip in sin. I should know better
than to desire so freely, a precursor to *you get what you ask for.*
I am trying to understand God without conquest,
to unstitch savagery sewn into bodies like mine.

Missionaries telling us to kneel at the crucifix for Jesus
whiter than a communion wafer. To suffer as readily as rain,
that heavenly reward, a casket. How many lost as martyrs?
Days of praying, repenting for the sins of their skin.
Blackness, stigmata never touching holiness, outcast to purity.

Time has passed now, yes, but has the message? I don't think
myself faithless, but I'm searching for the gods my ancestors
knew without heathenry. Gods unwritten, who do not rely
on my ugliness to forgive me, that allow for the fullness
of myself; desiring, sometimes wicked and raging.

Can I ask these gods where they have been?

What should I bring to the altar of your feet?
Should I offer kola nut?
How can we speak (seeing as my English has always been
a lost currency)?
Would you remind me that your language is my language,
is a bridge that is broken?
Is there another way I might understand you?
Were you the gust of wind that pushed open my window
when I was bound in fever?
A divine breeze soothing the tip of my nose?
Or the book that slammed free from the shelf, to jolt me
from the shock of loss?
The bee who flew into my room, misplaced in the chill
of winter, hovering above my head?
Deep belly laughter swirling in the trunk of my stomach,
more sublime than I can give myself credit for?

Should I look for you in the small miracles of my days?
Like this, might I come to know you?

And what if death is not departure but a return?
A night bus home at the end of a long day,
heading towards a house
dark but for one room with the light on?

WHEN THE PARTY IS OVER

In memory of Belly Mujinga, Christopher Kapessa,
Shukri Abdi and many more

Blackface

another terror, distorted
reflection in a fairground mirror.

For some, savage play, the costume afro,
smeared mud ritual and growl;
revelling in their rage, the spectacle
of wickedness absorbed by blackness,

for others the finger wag and tongue pop,
edges and box braids, melanin in makeup,
contoured and juicy, twerk of the party
shows me I'm telling my story all wrong.

I watch them run away with our effigies,
knowing it is only a matter of time
before someone spits venom in one of our faces
or a child is found face down in a riverbed.

Everyone else disappears when the party is over,
our bodies trampled on and tossed back to us.

WE'RE NOT HIRING MANY BLACK GIRLS THIS SEASON

too much sass. bad attitude. jezebel. ink blot. too much chunk. ratchet. coming for you. too much *They just don't have the right aesthetic*. too much spice. juice. thick lip. nappy knot. ink blot. baartman bounce. curves. suffocating you. too much. *We're following what sells*. too much temptress. wild. jungle-fever bite. heat. vulgar fantasy. secret crotch creep. silent shudder. wet. too much bruise. wanton and deserving it. an ink blot spoiling the clothes. too much. *We're going for a very specific look*. too much choke. animal. rage. hip jut. grit. overspill. cheap sell. deviant. spoiling the clothes. an ink blot spoiling the clothes. too much *European*. *These girls tend to have fewer curves*. Keep it Simple Unsoiled Neat Keep it Straight Whip Straight Tame Flowing Keep it Clean Pure Snow Chaste Keep it Clear Elegant Flowing Mild Keep it Chic Keep it Classic Current Keep it Perfect Keep it Now. Keep it.

13.42

Somehow your tears have
become the rain whipping
outside the glass and like with all things
delicate, I am afraid to touch you.
We're on the slow train
Euston to Birmingham, booked
as lovers. But today we are juddering
into each and every village stop
calling at Banbury and Dorridge
the background a tableau
of flitting elegies; bleeding rivers,
skies burdened and overcast,
boggy marshes, sinking,
beauty that hurts to watch.
A passing couple give us
the embers of their laughter
and I would think this spite
had they not already gone,
left us here in this carriage
with nowhere to look but
the window, a coffee cup
stain and wayward crumb
before back to each other,
knowing it's only a matter
of time before we reach
our final stop, eventually.

WE HAVE EVERYTHING WE NEED

We have each become a small world,
spinning from one collision to another.
We scrub cities off our skins and watch
their roads leave tracks in the bath.

Damp rises, rent rises, high-rises.
Look how the cities' silhouettes grow
new forests for us. What bright constellation
of stars guides us home?

We are tower-block light-flickers
come evening, crammed into shoeboxes,
basements, living room-cum-bedrooms.
Stretch out our feet to turn the TV on.

We reach for our phones, our faces made radiant
by their birdsong. Someone somewhere is mining
for the next iPhone but we can't be sure,
we are compassion in 280 characters.

We are lying lonely next to each other
between paper-thin walls. We know
our neighbours' shouts and moans,
an echo chamber of coughs and scrapes.

Rent rises, heat rises, sea rises.
Put the kettle on, burn dinner in microwaves.
Droughts happening somewhere, but we can't be sure,
Tesco fluorescence – open twenty-four hours.

I wonder what will this all look like in fifty years' time.
How will our cities exhale then?
How will we wear our loss?
How will we sleep when we cannot turn off the alarm?

UNSPEAKABLE THINGS

Every session, the physio finds new ways
to massage unspeakable things
out of my frame. The repetition of
You're so angry! a crick in my neck,

another black death, a shawl of lead knots
weighing on my posture, and where his love
should have been, a walnut fused
between the crests of my shoulders.

His last words continue to crack
in the physio's hands at the base of my spine,
vertebrae clinging onto its memory.
She keeps coming back to its vibration.

I have stopped talking. My platitudes
make mockery of the sinews of grief
twisting the shape of me. So, I lie there
silent, a cold body under forensic light.

ONE YEAR

I fear if I get out of bed
on a day like today
each footstep will turn the floor linoleum,
the smell of bleach
returning to calcify my nostrils.
I'll draw open my curtains
onto the ward
and be engulfed by the Morse code
babble of machinery.
My watch will tick like the clock
on the hospital wall
and my wondering *when*.
If I see my reflection
I'll find his face
in the mirror
blanched and drooping.
Even my bed is becoming bound
by the precision
of two sharp hospital corners,
the duvet crinkling
like a foil blanket.
So I give in to the day,
stand in my room,
the hospital,
and wait for him to die again.

CONVERSATIONS AT THE BUS
STOP: PIE AND MASH

There was something about the hospital ward on the day he died, where the thought, *why my father over them?* did cross my mind. There were no private rooms available. Instead, we were surrounded by elderly men watching *Countdown*, their coughs guttural and distraught. One patient had a spine riddled with rust. He was so gnarled and bent over, living at half-mast. Another was already a funeral. He lay there, grey as the sheets, limbs soft and confused, slowly sinking into the mattress. I tried not to stare at the granddad chewing on a jelly baby for a good hour, sticky resin in the corners of his mouth. *Why my father over them?* I would have definitely put money on some of them dying first. But death isn't always logical like that. And you can unravel yourself trying to find order in it, yet marathon runners can die a stunned death, sometimes with no warning at all. He died on that ward with the curtains drawn. Did those men still do their crosswords while hearing the last of everything and then nothing? Was *Countdown* still on or had we moved to *A Place in the Sun*? I couldn't hear anything else. He was still on record for dinner, the nurse rolling his pie and mash on a trolley towards us. *Oh!* she whispered as she opened the curtains, tray in hand, to find us scattered around him, debris of a quiet bomb. I wonder if someone else ate the food or if the plate was left back on the kitchen counter, gravy congealing, the mash clammy and cold.

MANGO TREE

Mother, you are cutting that mango with a chainsaw.
Its teeth have left it with a coat of angry track marks
and yet it remains a closed fist. You bought the mango
too soon, ignored the insolence of its skin,
thought you could carve it a better name.

The summer we flew back to your favourite mango tree
we found it as you'd left it; fruit overladen,
branches benevolent. I ran to your stride
as you retraced your footsteps back
to the ribcage of the tree. You shook its girth

until the most fickle of mangoes lost their will,
golden grenades surrounded our feet.
You sliced the best one with a skilled deftness,
mango juice down your fingers, you laughed
as my eyes willed to taste. *That laugh*

as if fallen from the tree, luscious and oozing through
blushed skin, full of fat pulp, glistening under sun,
sweet on my lips. We sat under the mango tree
and you spoke to me in Igbo and mango. Its strings lodged
between my teeth for the rest of the day.

Back here you are a sculptor trying to sigh life
into this cold boulder. It stays prude and indifferent
to the sharpness of the blade. I watch its anaemic curls
wizen into northern air, see how it leaves
bitter secrets in the hollow of your mouth.

I miss your laugh.

ANOTHER LENS

When I took out your lens
and put in my own, I found
tapestries unfurling over
continents. I saw dashiki
and denim, black-blue shine,
the swing of fresh braids
damask kisses. I saw soft
belly over jeans, lips thick
and wide, cropped ankara
and trainers. I saw a low tide
of broad noses, fresh fade,
eyeliner flick, kufi cool, scuffed
brogues, sky bouquets of curls.
I saw bow tie and braces,
red lip shine, butterfly locs.
Shaved head shimmer,
curve and bounce, dip
and wind, Supermalt swig,
sharp suit, sharper tongue.
I saw twist out boasts, sky
bun, amazon strut, peacock
posture, broad shoulder tops,
side plait sweep, headwrap
sculptures. I saw people
with laughter spilling out
of their mouths, refracting
and bouncing off the glow
of their skin, the depth
of their skin, the courage

of their skin, till there was
so much joy. Overflowing,
messy and warm. I took
out your lens and put in
my own. It made you feel
uncomfortable. I liked that.

BACK FROM THE DEAD

Maybe it should come as no surprise
that Lazarus grows turmeric on his farm
in Bodo. Given his namesake in the Bible
was brought back to life, how apt
that Lazarus should speak of rebirth,
bringing Ogoni soil back from the dead.
Turmeric grows in defiance of neighbouring
lands, fallow and bereft but for oil welts
slick with stagnancy. Nothing destined
to survive. But for Lazarus, a harvest
of golden root, gnarled resilience, living.
Turmeric, a blessing that soothes
and heals, despite its bitter taste.

EVERYTHING IS EVERYTHING

I was always taught
that one hand washes the other,
two dancers moving instinctively
fingers mirroring and intertwining
underwater. So then, let us understand
how we all move together;
how a seed has to know the soil
to become itself. The way many crops
only ripen into bud when a bee
seeks them. The rain must come,
as must the sun, the weather offering
a lesson in what it means to persevere
both in shadow and in light. All this,
tended by a farmer's wisdom,
learning just when to sow, rear, pluck.

We are eating from a whole world.

And we, once seed, return
back to the earth, giving life
to the soil and who knows
what might grow in our memory?

CAROUSEL

I cannot have my father die in front of me again,
will not survive living in the agony of his hospital bed.

Instead, I fill my head with the flowers my love gave me,
in the garden of my mind, I let them grow wild.

I'll travel in the memory of the first time he said he loved me
sit on its carousel and pass through it again;

How he offered those words, like jewels, and I hung them
softly around my neck. I will twirl around and around

the electricity, the promise in how he held my hand,
tender. I will fling open my arms, let the joyride take me

and who knows what else I'll find in the merry-go-round?
How did our feet talk? What taste our first kiss? For every turn,

a new colour. It doesn't matter what came next, just a moment,
a lifetime, and me laughing with a head full of flowers.

A LITTLE RESURRECTION

There are no last names for the women
who plait your hair early on a Saturday.
The women who know when you say
first thing you mean *first thing* – but still try
and do a quick weave beforehand –
need only be known by their first names.
So, call for Esther, Amina and Barbara,
their voices reverberating off the tired walls
of shops with faded signs. Look for their hot irons
standing to attention, the collection of oils
and creams, and pictures in the window
showcasing an array of hairstyles,
any of which the women will turn their hand to.
Ask them where sells the freshest fish,
who can thread your eyebrows for the best price,
which aunty gives extra maths tuition for the young.
Listen to the cross-examination of local gossip,
cackled anecdotes in four different languages.
Let them orbit the globe of your scalp
as they tug through knots with a wide tooth
and braid the weight of their histories
into your hair, leaving you with a pinched halo
of pain. These women do not care
for last names, but will give you the curve of their hip
to lean on mid-style, will hand over their baby
while they buy more hair for you, before returning
to the sounds of their child babbling on your lap.
Make no mistake, this is neither sentimental nor loving.

This is the unspoken kinship of the not-quite-safe-
on-this-island, those with bodies made so foreign
and ungodly for this country to bear, we do not realise
we are running on half breath until we sit down,
and then see how the women need only offer
the attention of their hands to give us some grace.
Call this a little resurrection, the making of a new crown,
a few hours to look in the mirror and be beautiful.

NEVER MINE

I see you walking towards me on Waterloo Bridge
and I could say hello, but instead let you pass by.
Time knows we are not the people we once were
and I have no strength to revive old ghosts.
There are holes in my laughter now, and for you
to notice this is another shame I can't stand.
Besides, I buried the words I should have given you
years ago, only visit the grave in the panic of night,
barefoot and lonely. And anyway, didn't I learn
long before now that growing up is other people
you can't have? That you were beautiful but never
mine to love? So, I throw the couple we would have been
in the Thames, watch the mirage sink slowly,
without struggle, until the backs of our heads
become small as two coins, and I keep walking.

REPLAY

When a woman flirts with you at a party, you think
how flattering as you try to fish the gaze of a man
who will not learn your name. Later, you will
replay the night like a tape in your mind's eye.

Play. How she stroked your cheek. *Pause.*
Rewind. The way her eyes tripped over
your mouth. *Play.* Why did opening my lips
feel like breaking bread? *Stop. Fast-forward.*

Later still, you will notice how the wind
wins a fight with a friend's headband
and makes theatre out of her hair,
each strand beckoning applause

or the sprinkle of freckles on a bartender's face,
wonder how many constellations you could
trace with the tip of your finger as she smiles
and adds an extra wink of gin to tonic.

Afterwards, the contours of her dress, the plunge
at its back a glittered invitation into the base
of her spine, how when she dances the zip
becomes a question mark this night cannot resolve.

You will notice that you're noticing.

You will wonder whether you have spent
your whole life unaware of your longing, trapped
in thistle and barbed wire

rewinding and replaying each lost chapter
and the love there could have been.

CORDS THAT CANNOT BE BROKEN
For Nawi Collective

I am forever grateful for the company
of black folk and our ability to dance
surrounded by flames. How at home

I am in the company of our laughter,
generous and extravagant. One evening
someone, in jest, starts to sing

Bind us together, Lord and without hesitation
the rest of us rise to our feet, all singing in unison.
What a gift to be your own church,

ready to give thanks for the constancy of your being.
Harmony, filling the room
with *Bind us together, Lord, bind us together.*

Children of the faithful, of parents
travelling continents, clinging to the cross
for protection and our tongues an heirloom

carrying the continuum of time;
Sunday School ritual, greased hair
and freshly ironed clothes buttoned too tight.

Later, for some, the questioning,
stepping out of holy light, the unsung
tune of what belief remains now,

the worship we have long since lost –
but what else is blackness but a chorus
of both praise and grief in one note?

I bring my mother to the song, the way
she sings hymns like this one, loudly,
a lifeline – prayer for times better than these.

I hum her faith into the melody,
weave her trust into the *cords*
that cannot be broken and I pass it along.

CONVERSATIONS AT THE BUS
STOP: PINK FURRY SLIPPERS

I wore my pink furry slippers in the aftermath. Mourners eyed
them on entering the house and I'd like to think it was for my
fearless fashion statement over it being a wholly inappropriate
option. Handy, should you find yourself running back to your
old town with only the clothes you're wearing and the relics
of your youth for a wardrobe. A joke gift, the kind you should
probably grow out of before too long; obscene tufts of shaggy
fushsia, shocked and standing to attention, four claws on each
foot, outstretched and jester-like. Very comfortable though.

The slippers cackle in the living room at my father's wake.
Heckling as we sit there, heads in hands –

*Erm, hello? Is this supposed to be a party? C'mon! Who went
and died? Oh right, well . . .*

While picking hymns with the vicar for the service –

*Wow . . . so you really mean to say that any one of us could go at
any time, huh? No wait, there's really no guarantee anyone will
find the meaning we're all searching for? Whew, I guess we'd cry
too. Drinks anyone? Vicar, lovey, what's your pleasure?*

When we are picking the colour scheme for the flowers,
sighing over orchids, the slippers chip in –

*Do you think flowers are going to stop anyone from dying alone,
babes?! Bitch, you better be serious!*

It's amazing, really, when you think about them. The frivolous comperes no one asked for.

You can see why I've kept them.

REPATRIATION IV

If it isn't clear in the living,
where do the dead belong?

My father takes his last breath
in England and is buried
in Nigeria on a clear blue sky
despite the odds of rainy season.
Seeing his coffin gives permission
to witness his life whole and I can see
the boy in the man. A different
pain, to understand a parent
fallible and afraid, just like you.
Death no epiphany, just a fade-
out while the rest of us continue
to shallow-breathe. The red clay
soil, land I have barely trod upon,
his rest, and this is his return,
going back to where he came from.
I have nothing more to inherit.

ANOTHER COUNTRY

So we left. Every single one of us
who'd ever been told to leave the country – gone.
No one stopped to look at the carcass we left behind.

I'd be lying if I said I knew where we all ended up,
whether this is a happy story.

The month I lived in Dakar
a shy artist admired the bloom of my skin,
how much darker I was becoming
under the sun. A flower finally flourishing.

A year later he told me he missed me
in English – not his mother tongue –
so he could be sure I understood
and the sun shone back on my face.

I'd like to live in that feeling –
if I could turn it into another country, I would.

A Note on Resurrections

Repatriation I – Despite never having been to Iraq, Jimmy Aldaoud was deported there from the US, as part of the ongoing ICE deportations of Iraqi communities. With mental health issues and a limited supply of insulin for his diabetes, Jimmy died sixty-three days later and was brought back to be buried in the US

Repatriation II – Written in response to the tragedy in which thirty-nine Vietnamese people froze to death inside a lorry in Grays, Essex in 2019

Prayer for the Deported – Inspired by the research of Luke de Noronha, author of *Deporting Black Britons: Portraits of Deportation to Jamaica* and producer of the podcast *Deportation Discs*

We're Not Hiring Many Black Girls this Season – Valentino's 'African'-themed Spring 2016 show featured bongo-style drumming and had models in cornrows wearing bone necklaces, feathers and safari prints. Eight out of the show's eighty-seven looks were given to black models

Back from the Dead – Inspired by the blog, 'Of Turmeric and Truth: "Fuel for Thought" and the struggle in Ogoni', by Andy Rowell (Oil Change International) and James Marriott (Platform) who write about Lazarus Tamana, Europe Co-ordinator of the Movement for the Survival of the Ogoni People (MOSOP). Lazarus grows turmeric on his land despite ongoing ecological devastation and damage from oil spills in Ogoni, Niger Delta

Cords that Cannot Be Broken – Taken from the hymn 'Bind Us Together, Lord'

Acknowledgements

A number of these poems were originally featured in the following journals and publications: *Magma* (issues 73, 81 and 82), *Where We Find Ourselves* (Arachne Press), *More Fiya* (Canongate Books) and *Keep the Bodies Buried* (The African Poetry Book Fund/Akashic Books).

Several poems were commissions by the former ACE Hotel Shoreditch, the Royal Society of Arts (RSA), In Place (a collaboration between Brunel University, Beyond Borders, Sound and the Arts Council), Wellcome Trust and the Institute of Contemporary Arts (ICA).

Financial support was gratefully received from the Society of Authors and the Authors' Foundation.

I am so thankful for the guidance and encouragement I have received from everyone who has supported my poetry and this book, with special thanks to Maya Goodfellow, Désirée Reynolds, Lola Okolosie, Mariam Hussain, Nova, Almir Koldzic, Sai Murray, Grace de Morgan, Louise Foreman, Annie Cross, Hannah Lowe, Crystal Mahey-Morgan and Kayo Chingonyi.